WESTMINSTER WORDS

WESTMINSTER WORDS

Wit and Comment from Both Houses of Parliament

GREG KNIGHT, MP
and
STEPHEN PARKER

Illustrated by Ian Nuttall

BUCHAN & ENRIGHT, PUBLISHERS

First published in 1988 by
Buchan & Enright, Publishers (Fountain Press Ltd)
45 The Broadway, Tolworth, Surrey KT6 7DW

British Library Cataloguing in Publication Data

Westminster words : wit and comment from
  both Houses of Parliament
  1. Humorous prose in English, 1945 - –
  Anthologies
  I. Knight, Greg   II. Parker, Stephen
  828'.91407'08

  ISBN 0-907675-88-3

Photoset in North Wales by
Derek Doyle & Asssociates, Mold, Clwyd
Printed in Great Britain by
Biddles Ltd, Guildford, Surrey

To the memory of Isabel Knight

INTRODUCTION

This is not a typical political book, as most politicians enjoy writing about themselves, and I have not done so. Usually, but not exclusively, those who have held office go into print with their version of events – it would seem that one of the by-products of a democracy is the 'kiss and tell' – or in some cases the 'abuse and tell' – memoir, the motive for which may be money, but is usually the settling of some old scores.

This book is not supposed to fall into either of these categories. I do not (yet) have any old scores to settle.

It was during the course of a particular debate, which had had a soporific effect on most MPs present, that I heard a verbal gem from the MP addressing the Chamber. Much to my astonishment, the remark went unnoticed and I began to wonder how many other shafts of wit had, over the years, been lost to posterity. I was considering writing an article on the subject when I met Stephen Parker, and the two of us hit upon the idea of this book.

The one thing that has continued to motivate us is that putting *Westminster Words* together has been fun.

Listening, observing and researching has convinced us that Jonathan Swift was right when he said 'proper words in proper places make the true definition of style'.

Most people, not just politicians, have at some time overheard a conversation, or have been impressed with some witty repartee, and have thought 'I wish I'd said that'. This book is a collection of some of the most memorable remarks made by MPs and Peers over the centuries. Some of the comments are witty, some vicious, some even banal, but all are, I believe, of interest.

Although you may have heard some of the comments before, particularly a few of those made by Winston Churchill, we have been careful not to put together a collection of old chestnuts. Many of the words quoted have not appeared in a collection before.

However, all of the contents, whether serious or light-hearted, confirm in our view the comments of Rudyard Kipling, when he said: 'Words are the most powerful drug used by mankind'.

GREG KNIGHT
House of Commons
October 1988

LORD ALTRINCHAM (1924-   )

Autobiography is now as common as adultery, and hardly less reprehensible.

LORD AMULREE (1900-1983)

It is more likely that adultery will be commited if people are living in cramped conditions.

LORD ARDWICK (1910-   )

Those of us who are veterans of Fleet Street recall a situation in the 1930s. At that time, there used to appear in the dock, at least once a week, some thief or confidence trickster, and very often he would describe himself as an Old Etonian – an Etonian of no fixed abode. He never described himself as an Old Wykehamist or Harrovian, perhaps because the words were more difficult to pronounce, or because he thought that they would not fit into the headlines. But he also described himself as a journalist, and this worried a number of journalists who were longing for respectability and for a professional place in society, just like doctors and lawyers.

MARGOT ASQUITH (1864-1945; WIFE OF H.H. ASQUITH, LATER LORD OXFORD AND ASQUITH, A LIBERAL PRIME MINISTER)

On Lloyd George: 'He could not see a belt without hitting below it.'

On the Labour politician Sir Stafford Cripps: 'Sir Stafford has a brilliant mind until it is made up.'

On F.E. Smith (later Lord Birkenhead): 'He is very clever, but his brains go to his head.'

When visiting Hollywood, the actress Jean Harlow asked Margot Asquith about the pronunciation of her christian name. She replied: 'The T is silent, as in Harlow.'

And on her own husband, Herbert Asquith: 'His modesty amounts to a deformity.'

NANCY, LADY ASTOR (1879-1964)

HECKLER (during a political meeting): 'Say Missus, how many toes are there on a pig's foot?'

LADY ASTOR: 'Take off your boots, man, and count for yourself.'

For a long time Lady Astor was ignored by her fellow MPs. She had known Winston Churchill for many years, and so she asked him for a reason for this cold-shouldering. He said that a woman's presence in the House of Commons was as embarrassing as if she had come into his bedroom when all he had to defend himself with was a sponge. To which she replied:

'You are not handsome enough to have worries of that kind.'

Jimmy Thomas, the Labour Member, was staying at the Astor family home, Cliveden, when he was asked by Nancy Astor what topic he would choose if he were invited to speak there.

THOMAS: 'How about my telling them what the Labour Party, if it gets into power after the war, intends to do with the Cliveden estate?'

LADY ASTOR: 'My own suggestion is that you turn it into a boarding house and make me the landlady; though in that case, Mr Thomas, you'll have to pay for your board, a thing you've never done in the past.'

Asked at one of her meetings a question about police arrests of young women in the streets:

'I must tell you something awfully funny that happened to me in London the other day. I saw a young American sailor outside the House of Commons. I said to him, "Would you like to go in?" and he said, "You're the sort of woman my mother warned me against".'

I went to Admiral Sims that night, and said to him, "Admiral, you have one perfectly upright young man in the American Navy".'

The following altercation with an Irish heckler took place at one of Lady Astor's public meetings:

HECKLER: 'Go back to America!'

LADY ASTOR: 'Go back to Lancashire, you don't

belong to Plymouth.'

HECKLER: 'I'm an Irishman.'

LADY ASTOR: 'I knew it. I knew you were an imported interrupter.'

HECKLER: 'If I'd imported you, I'd drown myself in the sea.'

LADY ASTOR: 'More likely in drink!'

HECKLER: 'I don't drink.'

LADY ASTOR: 'Well, go and have a drink today, it might sweeten you.'

Public life is in some ways a nuisance, in some ways a privilege. It is a privilege to say what you like without being afraid of losing your job.

One of Lady Astor's main opponents in the Labour Party was a Mr W.T. Gay, a man of pacifist tendencies, of whom she had this to say:

'Mr Gay represents the shirking classes, I represent the working classes. If you can't get a fighting man, get a fighting woman.'

What would we say if men changed the length of their trousers every year?

LORD ATTLEE (CLEMENT ATTLEE, 1883-1967)

Sir David Maxwell-Fyfe, MP met Mr Attlee, as he then was, on the platform of Westminster Underground, on the same day that the latter succeeded George Lansbury as leader of the Labour Party, a position which was clearly going to prove both onerous and troublesome. Murmured Attlee:

'Yes, I am accepting condolences.'

A story is sometimes told about Clement Attlee, when, as Prime Minister, he met the Chinese Ambassador:

'I love Chinese food,' Attlee is alleged to have remarked.

Showing considerable interest in these remarks of the then British Prime Minister, the Chinese Ambassador replied:

'I am very pleased to hear that, Sir. What is your favourite dish?'

To which Attlee replied:

'Number 27.'

Democracy means government by discussion, but it is only effective if you can stop people talking.

LORD AVON (SIR ANTHONY EDEN, 1897-1977)

To be criticised is not necessarily to be wrong.

STANLEY BALDWIN (LATER LORD BALDWIN OF BEWDLEY, 1867-1947)

The intelligent are to the intelligentsia what a gentleman is to the Gents.

During the climax of his famous attack on the Press lords, Lord Beaverbrook and Lord Rothermere, in 1931:

'What the proprietorship of these papers is aiming

Clement Attlee

at is power without responsibility – the prerogative of the harlot throughout the ages.'

On Lloyd George:
   'He spent his whole life in plastering together the true and the false and therefrom manufacturing the plausible.'

His Majesty's ministers are co-equal, but luckily, they are not co-eternal.

I would rather be an opportunist and float, than go to the bottom with my principles round my neck.

ARTHUR BALFOUR (LATER LORD BALFOUR, 1848-1930)

Discussing whether public men should read news-papers page by page: 'I have never put myself to the trouble of rummaging through an immense rubbish heap on the problematical chance of discovering a cigar-end.'

Of an opponent's speech:
   'There were some things in it meant seriously which were humorous, and there were others meant humorously which were serious.'

A comment upon a speech:
   'Asquith's lucidity of style is a positive disadvantage when he has nothing to say.'

Margot Tennant, who was later to marry Asquith, teasingly suggested to Balfour that he was so self-contained that he would not greatly mind if all his close women friends – Lady Elcho, Lady Desborough, one or two others, and herself – were all to die. Balfour paused, then replied:

'I think I should mind if they all died on the same day.'

FRANK HARRIS (the writer): 'The fact is, Mr Balfour, all the faults of our age come from Christianity and journalism.'

BALFOUR: 'Christianity, of course, by why journalism?'

It is unfortunate, considering that enthusiasm moves the world, that so few enthusiasts can be trusted to speak the truth.

If there is no future life, this world is a bad joke; and whose joke?

Democracy is Government by explanation.

Balfour's niece, Blanche Dugdale, once asked her uncle what he thought were the principles of Toryism.

BALFOUR: 'Do you think that a profitable speculation?'

NIECE: 'I don't care, I want to hear what you have to say about it.'

BALFOUR: 'I suppose the principles of common-sense, to do what seems to be right in a given case …'

NIECE: 'Suppose that instead of being born Uncle Robert's [Lord Salisbury's] nephew you had been Gladstone's son?'

BALFOUR: 'Then Gladstone would have cut his throat at an early stage.'

18

Balfour was once half an hour late for a speech he was to make. On arrival he strolled to the platform and barked out, with a slightly French accent which added a touch of ferocity to his words:

'I am half an hour late. It is entirely my fault. I do not apologise.'

Nothing should impede the truth save a substantial sum of money.

Talking in a public house off Fleet Street, describing how an influential group of people once tried to silence him on a controversial subject:

'The beasts dared to offer me a bribe of £50!'

Sounds of outraged feelings arose from those present. Balfour continued:

'Now, if they had offered me £500, that would have made all the difference.'

On standing for the first time for Parliament as a Liberal in South Salford, and being Roman Catholic, he was advised by the Roman Catholic clergy that his religion would not help him and that he had best be quiet about it. He retorted by opening his first speech thus:

'Gentlemen, I am a Catholic. As far as possible I go to Mass every day. This is a rosary' – taking it from his pocket – 'as far as possible I kneel down and tell those beads every day. If you reject me on account of my religion, I shall thank God that he has spared me the indignity of being your representative.'

TONY BENN, MP (FORMERLY LORD STANSGATE, 1925-   )

After being re-elected in a by-election: 'Having served in eleven Parliaments, it would be difficult to describe this as a maiden speech. It would be like Elizabeth Taylor appearing at her next wedding in a white gown.'

LORD BERKELEY (1800-1881)

After boasting that he would never surrender to a lone highwayman, it happened, when crossing Hounslow Heath one night, that his carriage was stopped by a robber, which reminded Berkeley of his promise. He challenged the man:

'You cowardly dog, do you think that I can't see your confederate skulking behind you?'

The highwayman quickly turned around, whereupon Berkeley shot him dead.

ANEURIN BEVAN (1897-1960)

Righteous people terrify me ... Virtue is its own punishment.

Bevan was often accused by his enemies of enjoying the company of the wealthy in a way which was not compatible with his Socialist ideals. Lord Beaverbrook, for example, once taunted him with the nickname 'Bollinger Bolshevik'. Bevan was unmoved by such attacks. He cheerfully admitted to 'slumming it in the West End' and said:

'Stand not too near the rich man lest he destroy thee – and not too far lest he forget thee.'

Attacking Florence Horsbrugh, the Minister of Education in the first post-war Conservative Government:

'I do not know what the Right Honourable Lady, the Minister of Education, is grinning at. I was told by one of my Honourable Friends this afternoon that that is a face which has sunk a thousand scholarships ...'

During the Second World War there was some move to censor certain sections of the Press. Bevan saw little need for such a step, remarking: '

'You don't need to muzzle sheep.'

The soul of democracy can never be fatally wounded for it is never wholly exposed.

Bevan was one of the most bitter critics of the Munich settlement in 1938:

'The suggestion is that people of my constituency, the colliers, the steel-workers and railwaymen, should offer their bodies as a deterrent to German aggression. There is one man over there' – pointing to Prime Minister Chamberlain – 'you could offer – offer him. Let the Conservative Party, if it is in earnest, call a Carlton Club meeting and get rid of the Prime Minister. He is the man upon whom Hitler relies; he is the man responsible for the situation.'

Stanley Baldwin

I have never regarded politics as the arena of morals. It is the arena of interests.

He once urged his leader in the Labour Party:
'Please don't be deterred in the fanatical application of your sterile logic.'

On the pre-war ruling classes in Britain:
'Political toleration is a by-product of the complacency of the ruling class. When that complacency is disturbed there never was a more bloody-minded set of thugs than the British ruling class.'

Bevan's hostility towards Winston Churchill lasted throughout his life:
'He mistakes verbal felicities for mental inspirations. A man suffering from petrified adolescence. He refers to a defeat as a disaster as though it came from God, but to a victory as though it came from himself.'
'The mediocrity of his thinking is concealed by the majesty of his language.'

Criticising the presence, in Churchill's National Government of 1940, of many Tory members who he considered had been appeasers of Hitler:
'It is not necessary to see the end of the race to know that some of the horses will never see the finish. We were doubtful of them when they came up to the starting-post. They looked broken-winded and knock-kneed and some even seemed to have the staggers ... The principle of coalition provides the hilt; it is the men who form the blade. We have a strong hilt, but a very blunt blade. It is Mr Churchill's job to sharpen it quickly.'

Seeing Churchill at the time of the Abdication in 1936, tears rolling down his cheeks and exclaiming: 'I never thought the time would come when a Churchill must desert his King', Bevan replied breezily, recalling Marlborough's desertion of King James II for the Dutch invader who became King William III:

'Oh, it's only the second occasion in history.'

Another of his favourite targets for attack was Neville Chamberlain, of whom he said:

'He looked on the Labour Party as dirt. The worst thing I can say about democracy is that it has tolerated the Right Honourable Gentleman for four and a half years.'

Of Attlee:

'He seems determined to make a trumpet sound like a tin whistle ... He brings to the fierce struggle of politics the tepid enthusiasm of a lazy summer afternoon at a cricket match.'

'When Labour leaders substitute the role of courtier for that of agitator they fail at both.'

ATTLEE: 'The Honourable Member [Bevan] is so adept at pursuing lines, he pursues them so far that he generally finds himself back where he started. He is apt to become airborne in the last five minutes of his speech.'

BEVAN: 'The Right Honourable Gentleman is usually sunk at the end of his.'

Accusing Attlee of being 'loyal to the point of self-effacement', when the latter's memoirs, *As It Happened*, were published, he remarked:

'It's a good title. Things happened to him. He never did anything.'

Of Walter Elliot, the Minister of Agriculture at the time:

'A man walking backwards with his face to the future.'

Of the young Harold Macmillan:
'He enjoys prophesying the imminent fall of the capitalist system and is prepared to play a part, any part, in its burial, except that of a mute.'

ERNEST BEVIN (1881-1951)

A Member of Parliament once remarked that 'Nye Bevan is his own worst enemy.' Ernest Bevin was heard to mutter:
'Not while I'm around, he isn't.'

LORD BIRKENHEAD (F.E. SMITH, 1872-1930)

Jimmy Thomas, a Labour MP notorious for not pronouncing his Hs, once complained of an ' 'orrible 'eadache'. Smith suggested:
'What you need, my dear chap, is a couple of aspirates.'

Horatio Bottomley congratulated Lord Birkenhead on his elevation to the Chancellorship, and added: 'Upon my soul, F.E., I shouldn't have been surprised to hear that you had been made Archbishop of Canterbury.'
'If I had,' replied the new Lord Chancellor, 'I should have asked you to come to my installation.'

'That's damn nice of you,' said Bottomley.
'Not at all, I should have needed a crook.'

Lady Wimbourne, when Smith had spelt her name
wrongly, said to him: 'How would you like it, Mr
Smith, if I mispelt your name?'
  'My dear Lady, there is scarcely any alteration you
could make which would not add to its distinction.'

The Government has turned its back on the country,
and now has the impertinence to claim the country is
behind it.

At an election meeting, F.E. suggested that a heckler
who was constantly interrupting him should take off
his cap when asking a question, to which the heckler
replied that he would take off his boots if necessary.
  'Ah, I'd knew you'd come here to be unpleasant.'

Woodrow Wilson, President of the USA, whom F.E.
disliked intensely, asked him what in his opinion was
the trend of the modern English undergraduate:
  'Steadily towards women and drink, Mr President.'

ANDREW BONAR LAW (1858-1923)

Churchill did not think much of Bonar Law as a
statesman, once writing of him in a letter: 'Most men
sink into insignificance when they quit office. Very
insignificant men acquire weight when they obtain it'.
Bonar Law's opinion of Churchill was a little less
harsh. When the War Office was under discussion,
Winston, asked to make up his mind whether to take
the War Office or the Admiralty, said jokingly, 'What

is the use of being War Secretary if there is no war?'
Bonar Law retorted:

'If we thought there was going to be a war, we would
not appoint you as War Secretary.'

LADY VIOLET BONHAM-CARTER (1887-1969)

Lloyd George's Government, accused of warlike
tendencies, fell in 1922. Bonar Law, the Conservative
leader, appealed for a mandate of 'tranquillity'. Violet
Bonham-Carter commented:

'We have to choose between one man suffering
from St Vitus's Dance and another from sleeping
sickness.'

LORD BRABAZON OF TARA (1884-1964)

Most of the silly things in history have been done with
the best of intentions.

HENRY, LORD BROUGHAM (1778-1868)

A lawyer is a learned gentleman who rescues your
estate from your enemies and keeps it himself.

JAMES BRYCE (LATER LORD BRYCE, 1838-1922)

Medicine is the only profession that labours incessantly to destroy the reason for its own existence.

JOHN BUCHAN (LATER LORD TWEEDSMUIR 1875-1940)

An atheist is a man who has no invisible means of support.

LORD BYRON (1788-1824)

Though I love my country, I do not love my countrymen.

GEORGE CANNING (1770-1827)

Nothing is so fallacious as facts – except figures.

Save, oh save me, from the candid friend.

LORD DAVID CECIL (1902-1986)

The first step to knowledge is to know that we are ignorant.

EARL OF CHATHAM (WILLIAM PITT, THE ELDER 1708-1778)

Youth is the reason of credulity; confidence is a plant of slow growth in an aged bosom.

When referring to the maxim that every man's home is his castle:
'The poorest man may in his cottage bid defiance to all the forces of the Crown. It may be frail – its roof may shake – the wind may blow through it – the storm may enter – the rain may enter – but the King of England cannot enter! – all his forces dare not cross the threshold of the ruined tenement.'

The parks are the lungs of London.

LORD CHESHAM (1916-   )

If I am misinformed, I have misinformed myself.

Sir Winston Churchill

LORD CHESTERFIELD (1694-1773)

That silly, sanguine notion ... that one Englishman can beat three Frenchmen, encourages, and has sometimes enabled, one Englishman, in reality to beat two.

The only solid and lasting peace between a man and his wife is doubtless a separation.

Most people enjoy the inferiority of their best friends.

Very ugly or very beautiful women should be flattered on their understanding, mediocre ones on their beauty.

Our prejudices are our mistresses; reason is at best our wife: very often heard indeed, but seldom minded.

If the multitude ever deviate into the right, it is always for the wrong reason.

The less one has to do, the less time one finds to do it in.

The manner of a vulgar man has freedom without ease; the manner of a gentleman has ease without freedom.

As fathers commonly go, it is seldom a misfortune to be fatherless; and considering the general run of sons, as seldom a misfortune to be childless.

If a fool knows a secret he tells it because he is a fool.

To govern mankind one must not overrate them.

We, my Lords, may thank Heaven that we have something better than our brains to depend on.

Advice is always welcome; and those who want it the most always like it the least

Wear your learning, like your watch, in a private pocket; and do not merely pull it out and strike it, merely to show that you have one.

In matters of religion and matrimony, I never give any advice, because I will not have anybody's torments in this world or the next laid to my charge.

When a man is once in fashion, all he does is right.

The vulgar only laugh, but never smile, whereas well bred people often smile, but seldom laugh.

There are but two objects in marriage — love or money. If you marry for love, you will certainly have some very happy days and probably some very uneasy ones; if for money, you will have no happy days and probably no uneasy ones.

SIR WINSTON CHURCHILL (1874-1965)

His comments on developing appendicitis during an election campaign in Dundee in 1922, in which he came bottom of the poll:

'In the twinkling of an eye, I found myself without office, without a seat, without a party and without an appendix.'

Sir William Joynson-Jicks, who was delivering a speech in the House of Commons, saw Churchill making movements of disagreement:
'I see my Right Honourable Friend shakes his head, but I am only expressing my own opinion.'
Answered Winston: 'And I am only shaking my own head.'

Churchill reserved one of his harsher strictures for Ramsay MacDonald:
'I remember when I was a child being taken to the celebrated Barnum's circus. The exhibit which I most desired to see was the one described as the "Boneless Wonder". My parents judged that the spectacle would be too revolting and demoralising for my youthful eyes. I have waited fifty years to see the "Boneless Wonder" sitting on the Treasury Bench.'

Also on MacDonald:
'We know that he has, more than any other man, the gift of compressing the largest amount of words into the smallest amount of thought.'

Seeing Sir Stafford Cripps walk through the Smoking Room of the House of Commons:
'There, but for the grace of God, goes God.'

Sitting opposite Sir Stafford Cripps, a strict vegetarian, at dinner, Churchill suddenly leant over to his hostess and, glancing mischievously at Cripps said:
'I am glad I am not a herbivore. I eat what I like, drink what I like ... and he's the one to have a red nose.'

Of Joseph Chamberlain: 'He likes the working classes; he likes to watch them work.'

Of Sir Samuel Hoare over the India Bill of 1935:
'The Secretary of State is like a cow who has given a good pail of milk – but has then kicked it over.'

Charles Masterman, MP, once said to Winston: 'I have a great admiration for [Keir] Hardie. He is not a great politician but he will be in heaven before either you or me, Winston.' To which Churchill replied:
'If heaven is going to be full of people like Hardie, well, the Almighty can have them to himself.'

When he was seventy-five, he was asked if he had any fear of death.
'I am ready to meet my Maker. Whether my Maker is prepared for the great ordeal of meeting me is another matter.'

Churchill's opinion of another's speech: 'Well, I thought it was very good. It must have been good, for it contained, so far as I know, all the platitudes known to the human race, with the possible exception of "Prepare to meet thy God" and "Please adjust your dress before leaving".'

A photographer who had come to get a birthday photograph of Churchill said to him: 'I hope, sir, that I will shoot your picture on your hundredth birthday.' Winston surveyed the photographer briefly:
'I don't see why not, young man. You look reasonably fit and healthy.'

'Would you like to tell our readers, sir,' a journalist asked him, 'what are the desirable qualifications for any young man who wishes to be a politician?'

Churchill put on his bulldog look, and everyone thought he was going to come out with something really profound.

'It is the ability to foretell what is going to happen tomorrow, next week, next month, and next year' – pause – 'and to have the ability afterwards to explain why it didn't happen.'

To a barber who asked him how he would like his hair cut:

'A man of my limited resources cannot presume to have a hair style. Get on and cut it.'

In December 1941, after Pearl Harbor, Churchill sent a very formal note to the Japanese Ambassador in London, informing him of Britain's declaration of war upon Japan. Commenting about it later:

'Some people do not like this ceremonial style, but when you have to kill a man, it costs nothing to be polite.'

In 1942 Churchill addressed the Allied troops in the Roman amphitheatre at Carthage, in North Africa:

'I am speaking from where the cries of Christian virgins rent the air whilst roaring lions devoured them. And yet, I am no lion, and certainly not a virgin.'

A senior naval officer complained that his service's role in the war was not in accordance with its great traditions:

'Well, Admiral, have you ever asked yourself what the traditions of the Royal Navy are? I will tell you in three words. Rum, Sodomy and the Lash.'

About the Yalta Conference of February 1945, in which the fate of post-war Europe was discussed between Stalin, Roosevelt and himself:

'I don't see any way of realising our hopes of World Organisation in six days. Even the Almighty took seven.'

We shape our buildings, and then our buildings shape us.

Of Attlee: 'He is a sheep in sheep's clothing.'

'Mr Attlee is a very modest man. But then he has much to be modest about.'

Politics are very much like war; we may even have to use poison gas at times.

In 1948 Churchill declared:
'For my part I consider that it will be found much better by all parties to leave the past to history, especially as I propose to write that history myself.'

'Trying to maintain good relations with the Communists is like wooing a crocodile. You do not know whether to tickle it under the chin or beat it over the head. When it opens its mouth you cannot tell whether it is trying to smile or preparing to eat you up.'

All I can say is that I have taken more out of alcohol than alcohol has taken out of me.

Once a woman MP turned on Churchill after a rather heated exchange. 'Mr Churchill, you are drunk,' she said.
'And you, madam, are ugly, but I shall be sober tomorrow.'

LADY ASTOR: 'If I were your wife, I'd put poison in your coffee.'

CHURCHILL: 'If I were your husband, I'd drink it.'

A new MP, Sir Alfred Bossom, had entered the House of Commons. Churchill remarked:

'Bossom? Bossom? What an extraordinary name ... neither one thing nor the other ...!'

As Churchill entered the Commons Tea Room one day, a group of young MPs began to talk about him among themselves. One of them observed that his walk was rather unsteady, while another said that his eyes seemed to be getting weak, since he always seemed to have difficulty reading his notes. Another member commented that the real problem was that the old man couldn't really remember facts and figures any more.

Churchill put his newspaper down and added, 'Yes, and they say he's getting deaf, too.'

When Churchill was a young subaltern an overpowering lady told him that she cared for neither his politics nor his moustache. 'Madam,' he replied, 'you are unlikely to come into contact with either.'

We are all worms, but I do believe I am a glow worm.

When someone told Churchill that his fly buttons were undone, he reassured them, 'Don't worry, dead birds don't fall out of their nests.'

Attlee once came across Churchill at the urinal in the House of Commons lavatory. On seeing him, Churchill moved to the furthermost end.

'Not in a friendly mood today, Winston?' asked Attlee.

'No, its just that every time you see something big

Edwina Currie

you want to nationalise it.'

At Queen Elizabeth's coronation Churchill found himself becoming increasingly hungry, and looked enviously at Queen Salote of Tonga, who he saw was accompanied by a page-boy.

'Well,' he observed, 'at least she brought her lunch.'

An appeaser is one who feeds a crocodile, hoping it will eat him last.

A fanatic is one who can't change his mind and won't change the subject.

Someone says it's a lie. That reminds me of the remark of the Irishman who said, 'There are a terrible lot of lies going about the world, and the worst of it is that half of them are true.'

When eagles are silent, parrots begin to jabber.

The English never draw a line without blurring it.

When I was young I made it a rule never to take strong drink before lunch. It is now my rule never to do so before breakfast.

When you have got a thing where you want it, it is a good thing to leave it where it is.

Politics are almost as exciting as war and quite as dangerous, although in war, you can be killed only once, in politics many times.

If a Prime Minister trips, he must be sustained. If he makes mistakes, they must be covered. If he sleeps he must not be disturbed. If he is no good he must be poleaxed.

I always avoid prophesying beforehand, because it is much better policy to prophesy after the event has already taken place.

It is a Socialist idea that making profits is a vice. I consider the real vice is making losses.

Towards the end of his career as a Member of Parliament, Winston became rather absent-minded. A young MP noticed that the great man was leaving the Members' Cloakroom with his fly-buttons undone. Not sure how to broach this delicate matter, the young MP commented 'The guard-house door is open, sir'.

Churchill replied: 'And tell me, was the sentry standing to attention, or was he lolling on a couple of sand-bags?'

KENNETH CLARKE, MP (1940-   )

If I had to say which was telling the truth about Society, a speech by a Minister of Housing, or the actual buildings put up in his time, I should believe the buildings.

LORD DENNING (1899-   )

Anything which lessens the confidence of the people in our system of justice is a great drawback.

I always come down on the side of publicity for judicial proceedings as one of the surest safeguards of the rule of law.

There is nothing like stating one's reasons in order to clear one's mind.

LORD DEWAR (1864-1930)

Nothing deflates so fast as a punctured reputation.

The road to success is filled with women pushing their husbands along.

Four-fifths of the perjury in the world is expended on tombstones, women and competitors.

Judge a man not by his clothes, but by his wife's clothes.

Lions of society are tigers for publicity.

Love is an ocean of emotions, entirely surrounded by expenses.

41

Minds are like parachutes: they only function when open.

A husband should tell his wife everything that he is sure she will find out, and before anyone else does.

Confessions may be good for the soul, but they are bad for the reputation.

It is only the people with push who have pull.

BENJAMIN DISRAELI (LATER LORD BEACONSFIELD, 1804-1881)

When I want to read a book I write one.

The author who speaks about his own books is almost as bad as the mother who talks about her own children.

Youth is a blunder, manhood a struggle, old age a regret.

On Lord Liverpool, as Prime Minister:
   'The Arch-Mediocrity who presides, rather than rules over a Cabinet of Mediocrities ... not a statesman, a statemonger ... Peremptory in little questions, the great ones he left open.'

You know who critics are? The men who have failed in literature and art.

If every man were straightforward in his opinions, there would be no conversation.

42

I am bound to furnish my antagonists with arguments, but not with comprehension.

Of an MP who was often out of his depth in debates:
   'He was distinguished for ignorance; for he had only one idea and that was wrong.'

On being informed of an illicit love affair of Palmerston's, and being advised that he should use the information to discredit the latter during an election:
   'Palmerston is now seventy. If he could provide evidence of his potency in his electoral address, he'd sweep the country.'

I have always thought that every woman should marry, and no man.

Asked to explain the difference between a misfortune and a calamity:
   'Well, if Mr Gladstone fell into the Thames it would be a misfortune, but if someone pulled him out it would be a calamity.'

The magic of first love is our ignorance that it can ever end.

The fool wonders, the wise man asks.

The best way to become aquainted with a subject is to write a book about it.

It is well known what a middleman is: he is a man who bamboozles one party – and plunders the other.

Every man has a right to be conceited – until he is successful.

Talk to a man about himself and he will listen for hours.

A majority is always the best repartee.

Imagination is too often accompanied by somewhat irregular logic.

When, once, Disraeli was commenting on John Bright's humble background, someone pointed out to him that Bright was entirely a self-made man.

Disraeli replied: 'I know he is, and he adores his maker.'

Once, when addressing a public meeting, he was interrupted by a heckler who shouted, 'Speak up, I can't hear you.'

Disraeli responded: 'Truth travels slowly, but it will reach you in time.'

When he was on his death-bed Disraeli, by then Lord Beaconsfield, was told that Queen Victoria wished to visit him. 'No,' he replied, 'it is better that she does not. She would only ask me to take a message to Albert.'

HUGH DYKES, MP (1939-   )

The following altercation took place in the House of Commons on 23 April 1986:

MR DYKES: 'As this applies to economic and political
      issues –'

MR DEPUTY SPEAKER (Mr Ernest Armstrong):
      'Order! The Honourable Member must address
      the House. I cannot hear what he is saying.'

MR DYKES: 'I am sorry, Mr Deputy Speaker. I was trying to decide which way to face.'
MR MARLOW: 'You always are!'
MR DYKES: 'I now realise that I should not have said that.'

NICHOLAS FAIRBAIRN, MP (1933-   )

During a debate on the proposal to add flouride to Britain's water suplies, this exchange took place:
MR FAIRBAIRN: 'Flouride is a potent catalase poison which is cumulative. Nobody on any side of the argument denies that it is toxic.'
MRS EDWINA CURRIE: 'Flouridation has been nothing but good. Anything is a poison if we take enough of it. Were we to. spreadeagle my Honourable Friend on the Floor of the House and poor absolutely pure H_2O into him, it would kill him, or anyone else subjected to that treatment, in hours.'
MR FAIRBAIRN: 'All the poison that my Honourable Friend suggested, I would happily take rather than be spreadeagled on the Floor of the House by her.'

Commenting about former Prime Minister Edward Heath in 1985: 'He has no place in the party. He has no future in Parliament. He has no place, for Parliament is a generous place; democracy is a generous thing. May I suggest he pursues his alternative career and conducts orchestras, since he does not know how to conduct himself.'

Benjamin Disraeli

TERRY FIELDS, MP (1937-   )

… It is difficult to keep my temper, let alone observe the proprieties of this place.

LORD FITT (GERRY FITT, 1926-   )

The more I listen to some of the comments in this House, the more I am convinced that this House is as far removed from Northern Ireland as the Sea of Tranquillity.

CHARLES JAMES FOX (1749-1806)

When a potential voter said 'Mr Fox, I admire your head but damn your heart', Fox replied, 'Sir, I admire your candour, but damn your manners.'

HUGH GAITSKELL (1906-1963)

Let us never forget that we can never go farther than we can persuade at least half of the people to go.

LORD GEORGE-BROWN (1914-1985)

Most British statesmen have either drunk too much or womanised too much. I never fell into the second category.

WILLIAM EWART GLADSTONE (1809-1898)

Selfishness is the great curse of the human race.

SIR ROBERT GRANT-FERRIS (LATER LORD HARVINGTON, 1907-   )

Whilst Deputy Speaker, during a debate on education, he said:
'Order! Sedentary interjections are rather indecent.'

LORD GRETTON (1902-1982)

In the General Election of 1935, Lord Gretton's Socialist opponent was a Mrs G. Paling. At one of her meetings, Mrs Paling shouted, 'John Gretton is a dirty dog.'
Gretton shouted back:

'That's as may be, but we all know what a dirty dog does to palings.'

LORD HAILSHAM (QUINTIN HOGG, 1907-   )

The Marquess of Salisbury (whose family name is Cecil) made an attack on Iain Macleod as Colonial Secretary, on which Hailsham commented:
'If I had to choose between Marquesses, I prefer the Queensberry to the Cecil rules, because the Queensberry rules at least prescribe it is unfair to hit below the belt.'

The Communist world teaches an extremely simple view of Jesus. According to the Communists, he simply did not exist.

Of the Labour Party today: 'Of genuine working men with experience of labour they seem to have relatively few. Their places have been largely taken by university graduates with a grievance against society which seems psycological in origin rather than to arise out of some hardship or injustice actually suffered.'

On politicians: 'A politician must be trustworthy and if he is found out telling lies, or if he is discovered in even small financial dishonesty, he can only bow himself out of public life.'

On lawyers: 'I would rather have too few lawyers than too many, as in the United States. Lawyers are indispensable to any civilised society but they have limitations and weaknesses and should not be too thick on the ground.'

On giving legal advice: 'The only advice to give intending litigants is to steer clear of litigation.'

The best way I know of to win an argument is to start by being in the right.

Justice is the first of the social services, and it behoves a wise nation to provide good justice.

What one has done spontaneously, it is never pleasant to repeat again to order.

The House of Lords exercises influence rather than power.

Playing safe is not always the wisest thing to do.

No myth which has widespread influence can be wholly false.

MARQUESS OF HALIFAX (1633-1695)

When the police contend for their liberty they seldom get anything by their victory but new masters.

A wife is to thank God her husband has faults; a husband without faults is a dangerous observer.

Education is what remains when we have forgotten all that we have been taught.

By the time men are fit for company, they see the objections to it.

The best qualification of a prophet is to have a good memory.

If the laws could speak for themselves, they would complain of the lawyers in the first place.

Some men's heads are as easily blown away as their hats.

If a man loves to give advice, it is a sure sign that he himself wants it.

DENIS HEALEY, MP (1917-   )

You can't go too far to catch votes.

SIR ALAN HERBERT (1890-1971)

A strong opponent of Lady Astor's temperance campaign, A.P. Herbert, an Independent Member, remarked:
'When Lady Astor starts a campaign to close the pubs it is called idealism. If I plead for the pubs to be kept open till midnight it is propaganda for the brewer.'

A highbrow is the kind of person who looks at a sausage and thinks of Picasso.

The conception of two people living together for twenty-five years without having a cross word suggests a lack of spirit only to be admired in sheep.

LORD HILL (1904-   )

Dr Charles Hill, the 'Radio Doctor', was a strong critic of Aneurin Bevan, Minister of Health in Attlee's post-war Government. He once remarked:
   'The end is Nye.'

LORD HOME OF THE HIRSEL (SIR ALEC DOUGLAS-HOME, 1903-   )

In answer to the question whether he thought he would ever become Prime Minister:
   'No, because I do my sums with matchsticks.'

There are few halts between Keynes and Marx.

I don't mind criticism; after all, you ask for it when you go into politics.

I remember having an exchange with a girl who worked for the BBC and I asked her if she couldn't make me look better on TV. She said No, because I had a head like a skull. So I said 'Hasn't everybody got a head like a skull?' and she said, 'No,' and that was the end of the conversation.

So far as politics is concerned, television is bound to be superficial. You have to deal with the most complicated issues in a very short time.

SIR ROBERT S. HORNE (1871-1940)

Speaking in Parliament while Ramsay Macdonald was Prime Minister, Horne said of Lloyd George's followers:

'For their prayers they say "We err and stray like lost sheep and the Leader of the Liberal Party is our shepherd and our crook".'

JACK JONES (1884-1970)

Nancy Astor, the first woman Member of the House of Commons, was herself a teetotaller and a keen advocate of temperance. During one such speech, looking in the direction of Jack Jones, a fellow MP, she referred critically to 'beer bellies'. Jones interrupted:

'I will tell the Noble and Honourable Lady that I will lay my stomach against hers any day.'

LORD KILMUIR (1900-1967)

Loyalty is the Tories' secret weapon.

Sir Anthony Eden

LORD KIMBALL (SIR MARCUS KIMBALL, 1928-   )

It always frightens me when the courts and the law see an insurance company and a claim. It is rather like a pack of hounds when they see their fox. The lawyers' tongues hang out and their wigs flow behind them as they brandish their sticks and pursue the wretched underwriter to a point where they can no longer carry on in business.

NEIL KINNOCK, MP (1942-   )

My only contribution to the war effort was in giving up bananas for the first three years of my life.

The sooner the Opposition acknowledges that public enterprise in this country, as everywhere else, has the choice of meeting its need for revenue by collecting from the Exchequer or by putting up its prices, and the sooner they face the political choice and the practical task unenviable as it may be, and face it honestly, the sooner will they make a great contribution to political and public education about the needs of public industry and of private industry.

Referring to war against an enemy armed with nuclear weapons: 'In those circumstances the choice is again posed ... of either exterminating everything you stand for ... or using the resources you've got to make any occupation totally untenable.'

HENRY LABOUCHÈRE (1831-1912)

I do not object to Gladstone always having the ace of trumps up his sleeve, but merely to his belief that God Almighty put it there.

Of course I think that our Party is right, but whether we are or not we've got the humbug on our side.

The mere denial of the existence of God does not entitle a man's opinion to be taken without scrutiny on matters of greater importance.

Believing that Queen Victoria should provide for her grandchildren out of her own income, and not from the public purse, Labouchère added an extra verse to the National Anthem:

> *Grandchildren not a few*
> *With great-grandchildren too*
> *She blest has been*
> *We've been their sureties*
> *Paid their gratuities*
> *Pensions, annuities*
> *God save the Queen!*

Labouchère once retailed a highly scandalous piece of gossip to a female friend. The lady, greatly disconcerted, at length exclaimed: 'I am sure, Mr Labouchère, you can't be talking of my cousin.'

   'My dear madam, surely you don't imagine that I would tell such a story outside the family?'

When Labouchère was at Cambridge a proctor

caught him one day walking with what was then called a 'lady of pleasure'. Coolly, Labouchère introduced her as his sister. The proctor was outraged. 'Nonsense! She is one of the most notorious courtesans in town.' The young Labouchère looked aggrieved:

'I know that, sir, but is it kind to throw my family misfortune in my face.'

A pompous nobleman called at the British delegation in St Petersburg and demanded to see the Ambassador at once. 'Pray take a chair; he will be here soon,' said Labouchère.

'But young man, do you not know who I am?' the nobleman replied, reciting his distinctions.

'In that case,' repied Labouchère, 'pray take two chairs.'

NIGEL LAWSON, MP (1932-   )

Commenting on the Liberals' decision in the 1970s to form the Lib-Lab Pact to maintain a Labour government in office: 'It is the only time in history that rats have been known to join a sinking ship.'

The Labour Party manoeuvres like a squid lost in its own ink.

The business of government is not the government of business.

DAVID LLOYD GEORGE
(LATER LORD LLOYD GEORGE, 1863-1945)

On Neville Chamberlain:

'He saw foreign policy through the wrong end of a municipal drainpipe. He might make an adequate Mayor of Birmingham in a lean year.'

On Sir John Simon, who left the Liberal Party to join the Tories:

'It is as if there are two types of men in this world, those who drink and those who do not, and it is as if the Right Honourable Gentleman has been a total abstainer all his life and has suddenly taken to drink and there he is; he swayed from side to side and landed amidst the Tory drunkards. The Right Honourable Gentleman has sat for so long on the fence that the iron has entered into his soul. Now, Mr Speaker, there have been many Honourable and Right Honourable Gentlemen greater than the Right Honourable Gentleman, who have crossed the floor of this house and have done so out of conviction, but never has an Honourable or Right Honourable Gentleman crossed it before and left behind him such a slimy trail.'

When Alfred Mond irritated him by his seeming adoption of Tory principles:

'I seized him by the tail, but it came off in my hand.'

In the House of Commons, Joynson-Hicks, the Convervative MP who had married an heiress and added his wife's maiden name, Joynson, to his own surname, poked fun at Lloyd George's phrase 'unearned increment'. He challenged the Welshman, then Chancellor, to explain what it meant; to which Lloyd George replied:

'On the spur of the moment I can think of no better example of unearned increment than the hyphen in the Right Honourable Gentleman's name.'

When introduced at a political meeting with the words, 'I had expected to find Mr Lloyd George a big man in every sense, but you see for yourself he is quite small in stature.'

'In North Wales we measure a man from the chin up. You evidently measure from the chin down.'

A politician is a person with whose politics you do not agree; if you agree with him he is a statesman.

In his early days Lloyd George was a great advocate of Home Rule, and wished to extend the principle to the Colonies. 'Home Rule for India, Home Rule for South Africa …' he called, during a speech.

'Home Rule for Hell,' shouted a heckler. 'That's right,' said Lloyd George, 'let everyone speak for his own country.'

On another occasion, Lloyd George's car broke down, and the nearest place to which he could go for help was a lunatic asylum. He knocked on the door and announced, 'I am the Prime Minister, may I come in?'

'Yes,' came the reply, 'The nearest Cabinet is waiting for you.'

With me, a change of trouble is as good as a holiday.

The most dangerous thing in the world is to try to leap a chasm in two jumps.

LORD MACAULAY (1800-1859)

Perhaps no person can be a poet, or even enjoy poetry, without a certain unsoundness of mind.

It is possible to be below flattery as well as above it.

We know of no spectacle so ridiculous as the British public in one of its periodical fits of morality.

The puritan hated bear baiting, not because it gave pain to the bear, but because it gave pleasure to the spectators.

From Byron they drew a system of ethics in which the two great commandments were to hate your neighbour and to love your neighbour's wife.

Few of the many wise apothegms which have been uttered have prevented a single foolish action.

LORD MANCROFT (1914-1987)

All men are born equal, but quite a few get over it.

Cricket is a game which the English, not being a spiritual people, have invented to give themselves some conception of eternity.

A speech is like a love affair. Any fool can start one,

but to end it requires considerable skill.

When being interrupted by a persistent heckler: 'A man with your intelligence should have a voice to match.'

LORD MANSFIELD (1705-1793)

Consider what you think justice requires, and decide accordingly. But never give your reasons; for your judgement will probably be right but your reasons certainly be wrong.

HARRY MARTEN (1602-1680)

During the Long Parliament which lasted throughout the Civil War, a member complained that those who fell asleep during debates should be got rid of. Harry Marten, who was well known for sleeping in the House, was aroused from his slumbers, and remarked:

'Mr Speaker, a motion has been made to turn out the nodders. I desire that the noddees may also be turned out.'

Cromwell once referred to Marten by mistake as Sir Harry Marten. Marten (again aroused from sleep) stood up:

'I thank Your Majesty. I always thought when you were King, I would be knighted.'

William Ewart Gladstone

REGINALD MAUDLING (1917-1979)

We all know that, as an election approaches, there is a temptation on both sides to maximise the differences between us and to try to escalate the condemnation of our opponents. That, in the nature of things, is inevitable, but it does not serve the public interest.

LORD MELBOURNE (1779-1848)

Lord Brougham once delivered a bitter diatribe against the Melbourne government. Melbourne answered thus:

'My Lords, you have heard the eloquent speech of the noble and learned Lord – one of the most eloquent he has ever delivered in this House – and I leave Your Lordships to consider what must be the nature and strength of the objections which prevent any Government from availing themselves of the services of such a man.'

I wish I was as cocksure of anything as Tom Macaulay is of everything.

DAVID MELLOR, MP (1949-   )

Commenting on another politician: 'She has a long reach, but a short grasp.'

Being even-handed does not mean that you need to treat people who behave differently in the same way.

LORD MORTON OF HENRYTON (1887-1973)

When a really troublesome question arises, the best way of dealing with it is to bury it in a Royal Commission.

SIR OSWALD MOSLEY (1896-1980)

When the first Labour Government came to power, Oswald Mosley was a young, up-and-coming Labour Member of Parliament. But he quickly became disillusioned by the government's timidity when Labour had at last attained power.

'What would you think of a Salvation Army which took to its heels on the Day of Judgement?'

SIR GERALD NABARRO (1913-1973)

Words surely have no meaning if they do not give a reply.

Of Michael Foot: 'His knowledge of industry could be accommodated on the back of a fourpenny stamp.'

Commenting on Albert Murray, the then Labour MP for Gravesend, he said: 'He is a mere flatulent lightweight.'

On former Prime Minister James Callaghan: 'It would be much better if he went to a secondary school evening class to learn to use a slide-rule.'

And commenting on himself: 'I am impotent – not in a physical, but in a parliamentary sense.'

DAVE NELLIST, MP (1952-   )

The solution to unemployment is the provision of jobs.

SIR HAROLD NICOLSON (1886-1968)

The Irish do not want anyone to wish them well; they want everyone to wish their enemies ill.

LORD NORTH (1732-1792)

One of Lord North's favourite tricks as Prime Minister was to pretend he was asleep during boring speeches from the Opposition benches in the House of Commons. On one occasion, an opponent exclaimed during a bitter speech against the government: 'Even now, in the midst of these perils, the Noble Lord is asleep.'

'I wish to God I was.'

LORD CHATHAM: 'If I cannot speak standing, I will speak sitting: and if I cannot speak sitting, I will speak lying.'
LORD NORTH: 'Which you will do in whatever position you speak.'

DAVID OWEN, MP (1938-   )

On being called a 'fellow-traveller' by the Conservatives: 'It is a far more potent libel for me than being accused of having it off with someone.'

There are times in politics when you should say 'never'.

LORD PAGET (REGINALD PAGET, 1908-　　)

Disgruntled by the lack of change in direction for the country and its government after the accession of Harold Wilson's Government to power in 1964, Paget complained in the House of Commons:

'I did not come here to substitute for an upper-middle-class Conservative government a lower-middle-class conservative one.'

LORD PALMERSTON (1784-1865)

Dirt is not dirt, but only matter in the wrong place.

The best thing for the inside of a man is the outside of a horse.

On his death bed:

'Die, my dear Doctor, that's the last thing I shall ever do.'

WILLIAM PITT THE YOUNGER (1759-1806)

Referring to a speech by Erskine:

'I shall make no mention of what was said by the Honourable Gentleman who spoke last. He did no more than regularly repeat what was said by the

Member who preceded him [Fox] – and regularly weakened all he repeated.'

Poverty of course is no disgrace, but it is damned annoying.

Don't tell me of a man's being able to talk sense; everyone can talk sense – can he talk nonsense?

Reading from a document from a body of army volunteers offering themselves for service, Pitt was shocked by the number of conditions and demands which they made. One such condition was that they should never be required to leave England; at which point Pitt wrote in the margin:
'Except in the case of actual invasion.'

Alluding one night to his small number of supporters for a Bill:
'I appear in the House of Commons as Eve in the garden of God – naked, yet not ashamed.'

HRH PRINCE PHILIP, DUKE OF EDINBURGH
(1921-   )

Dentopedalogy is the science of opening your mouth and putting your foot in it. I've been practising it for years.

ENOCH POWELL, MP (1912-   )

History is littered with wars that everybody knew would never happen.

All political careers end in failure.

Lord Hailsham

LORD JOHN RUSSELL (1792-1878)

Replying to Sir Francis Burdett, an ex-Radical who, attacking his former colleagues, had said, 'The most offensive thing in the world is the cant of Patriotism':

'I quite agree that the cant of Patriotism is a very offensive thing, but the recant of Patriotism is more offensive still.'

Among the defects of the Bill, which were numerous, one provision was conspicuous by its presence and another by its absence.

JOHN SELDEN (1584-1654)

Preachers say: do as I say, not as I do.

LORD SHERBROOKE (1811-1892)

On a friend remarking: 'I have the greatest contempt for Aristotle'.

'But not, I should imagine, that contempt which familiarity breeds.'

RICHARD SHERIDAN (1751-1816)

During a speech Sheridan referred to Gibbon as the 'luminous author of *Decline and Fall*'. Asked later why he had gone out of his way to flatter Gibbon, the playwright replied:

'Luminous? Oh, of course, I meant voluminous.'

When told that if he continued his heavy drinking he would destroy the coat of his stomach:

'Well then, my stomach must just digest in its waistcoat.'

TWO FRIENDS: 'I say, Sherry, we have just been discussing whether you are a greater fool or rogue. What is your opinion?'

SHERIDAN: 'Why, i'faith, I believe I am between both.'

When his son said that he intended to go into politics, but added: 'I will pledge myself to no party but write upon my forehead in legible characters, "To be let",' Sheridan replied:

'And under that, write "unfurnished".'

On the liberty of the Press, during a speech in the House in 1810:

'Give us a corrupt House of Lords, give us a venal House of Commons, give us a tyrannical Prince, give us a truckling Court, and let me have but an unfettered press, I will defy them to encroach a hair's breadth upon the liberties of England.'

On Warren Hastings:

'His crimes are the only great things about him, and these are contrasted by the littleness of his motives. He is at once a tyrant, a trickster, a visionary, and a deceiver. He affects to be a conqueror and law-giver, an Alexander and a Caesar, but he is no more than a Dionysius and a Scapin ... He reasons in bombast, prevaricates in metaphor and quibbles in heroics.'

An opponent said that he would like to knock Sheridan's brains out:
'You have heard my opponent's amiable desire. I have but one suggestion to make. Let him be very careful when he performs the operation. Let him pick up my brains, for he needs them sadly.'

Comments on a Ministerial speech:
'It contained a great deal of what was new and what was true, but unfortunately, what was new was not true, and what was true was not new.'

Sheridan obliquely accused the Secretary to the Treasury, John Robinson, of corruption, during a speech on Pitt's India Bill. It was a serious charge, and caused an uproar in the House. 'Who is it?' shouted Members, 'Name him! Name him! Name him!' Sheridan calmly turned to address the Speaker.
'Sir, I shall not name the person. It is an unpleasant individous thing to do. But don't suppose that I abstain because there is any difficulty in naming him. I could do that, sir, as easily as you could say "Jack Robinson".'

When a very ponderous Member stopped in the middle of a long, drawn-out speech to take a glass of water, Sheridan jumped up on a point of order. The Speaker asked him what the point of order might be:
'I think, sir, that it is out of order for a windmill to go by water.'

When the Whigs were defeated on a very unpopular Bill which they had introduced, Sheridan commented:

'I have often heard of people knocking their brains out against a wall, but never before of anyone building a wall expressly for the purpose.'

When a Speaker suggested that the Irish should be firmly suppressed, saying that there could be no strife where there was no opposition:

'True, just as there can be no rape where there is no opposition.'

Attacking Pitt's cabinet, pointing out that one Member, Dundas, held no less than three posts at the same time:

'If as has been stated, that gentlemen would serve their country better whilst at the same time serving themselves, we certainly have at present a most gentlemanly administration; and one gentleman, Mr Secretary Dundas, is three times as much a gentleman as any of them.'

EMANUEL SHINWELL (LATER LORD SHINWELL, 1884-1986)

Shinwell, a Labour MP, was on many occasions a strong critic of Churchill's wartime administration. A Churchill supporter said to him: 'You must remember that the Prime Minister is descended from Marlborough.' Shinwell, who was Jewish, replied:

'Please be so kind as to remind the Prime Minister that I am descended from an even older military leader – Moses.'

Those who preach Socialism fail to interest me.

When I entered Parliament, I was consoled, at any rate for a time, for my lack of education.

Leadership cannot be concentrated in any one person. It is a matter for collective wisdom.

However influential a Labour MP may consider himself, outside the House of Commons, he is of little consequence.

Nobody loves a free-for-all more than I do. To be independent and to do as one wishes is a delightful existence.

If power and authority were vested in myself, I would avoid war like the plague, but in the world as it is, defence, however costly, is essential.

DENNIS SKINNER, MP (1932-　　)

On the House of Commons: 'This is not the most important place in the world. We only react to events.'

As far as I am concerned, I have come to this House not to speak impartially, in the round, looking after everybody's interest. I have come here to speak for the miners, the working class, the trade unions and Labour movement, and no one else.

When the workers decide to stop work it is they who decide whether the economy will grow or stop growing.

I shall, for my own perhaps eccentric and personal reasons, continue to hold my views, whatever the result.

DAVID STEEL, MP (1938-   )

Looking back, there have been plenty of missed opportunites.

What I will look back on as my greatest achievement is simply the rise in support for the kind of policies that I've stood for.

I still hope and expect to be a member of government some day.

EARL OF STOCKTON (HAROLD MACMILLAN, 1894-1986)

On the tremendous reception given to Yuri Gagarin, the Russian astronaut who was the first man in space, during his visit to London:
   'It would have been twice as bad if they had sent the dog.'

Macmillan was sceptical of Harold Wilson's claim that when he was a schoolboy his family had not been able to afford to buy him any boots:
   'If Harold Wilson ever went to school without boots, it was merely because he was too big for them.'

In 1960, Macmillan was making an important speech at the United Nations in New York. Half-way through, he was rudely interrupted by Khrushchev, the Russian Premier, who took off one of his shoes and started banging the table with it. Macmillan remarked drily:

'I'd like that translated, if I may.'

I have never found, in a long experience of politics, that criticism is ever inhibited by ignorance.

His late son, Maurice Macmillan, former Conservative Member for Halifax, wrote a letter to *The Times* criticising the Government. Macmillan commented in the House of Commons:

'The Member for Halifax has intelligence and independence. How he got them is not for me to say.'

Pressing Hugh Gaitskell to disclose the Labour Party's plans for nationalisation, and not satisfied by Gaitskell's answer that steel and land transport were the only two industries to be taken over by the State:

'I will tell you the story of a poultry farmer, who one day was wandering round his farm when up spoke a turkey, who said to him, "Is it true that you are going to slaughter me?" The farmer replied, "My dear fellow, you can set your mind at rest. You see that bird over there and that bird over there? They are both on the list, but I have no plans for you at present." But it would be a very foolish bird indeed who took any comfort from that. Come Christmas, his neck will be wrung all right.'

It has been said that there is no fool like an old fool – except a young fool. But the young fool has first to grow up to be an old fool to realise what a damn fool he was when he was a young fool.

David Steel

As a young Conservative Member for Stockton-on-Tees, and often regarded as a rebel, attacking the Conservative Government Front Bench:

'Mr Disraeli once said that he saw before him a bunch of extinct volcanoes. I would not be so rude, but there are a few disused slagheaps which might well be tidied up.'

After hearing his Private Secretary, John Wyndham, complaining of the unnecessary danger involved in a wartime journey they were making in Algeria:

'All right, it'll be Wyndham and children first ...'

It is better to raise the level of the many than, by jealous and malicious policies, pull down a few.

Unemployment is not in itself a harmful thing. When it is unemployment of the upper classes it is called leisure. The real problem is that of not having enough money.

Conservatism has never become a temple for the preservation and worship of obsolescent doctrines.

The British economy, like the British weather, is apt to be variable.

Michael Foot made a bitter attack on me yesterday in the House of Commons, calling me a petulant and pathetic old man. He attacks everyone else with equal violence, so perhaps it could be said of him "everybody out of step except my Foot". There are three brothers. "One Foot is enough for me" is my motto.

The Conservative Party has always had the faith to honour the things that history has taught us to cherish and revere. But it also had the courage to grasp what is

78

new and fresh, so that a constant process of renewal takes place in our national life.

LORD STOW HILL (FRANK SOSKICE, 1902-1979)

There are some people, men or women, rich or poor, old or young, who are so abysmally stupid that they can neither read nor understand anything if you say it to them.

JAMES STUART (1885-1931)

When Secretary of State for Scotland, he was toiling through a long, boring, officially prepared statement in the Commons. A Labour MP shouted across the Chamber, 'Speak up!'
   'Oh, I didn't know anyone was listening.'

BARONESS SUMMERSKILL (1901-1980)

It has been said that men make the laws and women the manners.

MARGARET THATCHER, MP (1925-   )

Unlike Right Hon. and Hon. Gentlemen opposite, I could not be influenced to go back on an election promise.

Addressing the House on 5 February 1960, in her maiden speech, Mrs Thatcher said:
'I believe that is folly for any Hon. Member to lead the public into believing that there will be a fall in the absolute figures of Government expenditure. There will not be. It is almost certainly bound to rise, if only because the welfare services are expanding.'

We all know that there are difficulties in reducing public expenditure. The greatest hope for the future is to stop it from rising as fast as national income.

Speaking in a debate on the Queen's Speech in 1967:
'Civil servants have not got the expertise at their disposal which a merchant bank has. If they had such expertise, they would probably be working very successfully for a merchant bank.'

The single most important influence in a child's life is the parental influence.

Being powerful is like being a lady. If you have to tell people you are, you aren't.

If you've got a good thing to sell, use every single capacity you can to sell it.

We live in a television age, and television is selective.

It speaks louder than all of the statistics in Whitehall and Westminster. In today's world, selective seeing is believing.

We have to beware television dictating the political agenda.

Commenting on Lord Bowden, a former Labour Minister:
'As he had a very happy facility for putting his case cogently, it is not surprising that he did not last long as a Minister.'

If two people come out of college or school together and start in an identical job, with identical wages or salaries, they will finish their lives with wholly different wealth: one could save and the other spend.

I believe that capitalism and democracy are inseparable.

Of a Labour MP:
'The Hon. Gentleman suffers from the fact that I understand him perfectly.'

The price of new hope is persistent endeavour.

J.H. (JIMMY) THOMAS (1874-1949)

En route to the USA, at the usual last-night-at-sea party, Ramsay MacDonald made a speech and used a word usually denoted by an asterisk. At which his colleague J.H. Thomas exclaimed:

'And the asterisk of it is, 'e don't know what it means.'

JEREMY THORPE (1929-   )

Of Macmillan's Cabinet purge in 1962, the then young Liberal MP remarked:
  'Greater love hath no man than this, that he lay down his friends for his life.'

HORACE WALPOLE (LORD ORFORD, 1717-1797)

Since I am old and have the gout, I have turned those disadvantages to my own benefit and plead them to the utmost when they will save me from doing anything I dislike.

THE DUKE OF WELLINGTON (1769-1852)

When a lady remarked, 'What a glorious thing must be a victory, sir,' his reply was:
  'The greatest tragedy in the world, madam, except a defeat.'

Wellington was once approached by a stranger in the street and asked if he was Mr Smith.

'Yes, sir. And if you believe that, you'll believe anything.'

Nothing, except a battle lost, can be half so melancholy as a battle won.

The only thing I am afraid of is fear.

My rule always was to do the business of the day in the day.

Publish and be damned.

JOHN WILKES (1727-1797)

During a heated argument, the Earl of Sandwich remarked to Wilkes that he, Wilkes, would die either upon the gallows or of venereal disease. Wilks replied:
'That depends, my Lord, whether I embrace your principles or your mistress.'

An opponent of Wilkes once mused in his presence: 'I was born between twelve and one o'clock on the first of January, isn't it strange?'
'Not at all, you could have only been conceived on the first of April.'

During an election campaign, a heckler shouted, 'I would rather vote for the Devil than for John Wilkes.'
'And if your friend is not standing …?'

In his *Dictionary*, Doctor Johnson observed that 'h' seldom, perhaps never, begins any but the first syllable of a word.

Wilkes, who had not met Johnson but enjoyed baiting him from afar, took up the quotation in his newspaper, the *Public Advertiser*:

'The author of this remark must be a man of quick appre-hension and compre-hensive genius; but I can never forgive his un-handsome be-haviour to the poor knight-hood, priest-hood, and widow-hood, nor his in-humanity to all man-hood.'

LORD WILSON OF RIEVAULX (HAROLD WILSON, 1916-   )

During a visit to the United States, when asked what he considered were the main differences between himself and Macmillan:

'Twenty-two years.'

Attacking the Conservative Minister of Defence, Duncan Sandys, for what he considered to be the mistaken Blue Streak missile project:

'We all know why Blue Streak was kept on although it was an obvious failure. It was to save the Minister of Defence's face. We are, in fact, looking at the most expensive face in history. Helen of Troy's face, it is true, may only have launched a thousand ships, but at least they were operational.'

On Macmillan, during a House of Commons debate in 1958 (Wilson was the first to give Macmillan the nickname 'Mac the Knife'):

'Words for the Right Honourable Gentleman are like the false trail laid in a paper chase to cover up the way he is really going. It is when he has just been attacking the social services that he most likes to quote

Disraeli. I always thought Disraeli was one of his heroes until he went to Hawarden this year and made a speech about Gladstone. The Right Honourable Gentleman is the only statesman in this century to claim with characteristic modesty to embody all that is best in both Disraeli and Gladstone. In fact, of course, he is wrong. He has inherited the streak of charlantanry in Disraeli without his vision, and the self-righteousness of Gladstone without his dedication to principle.'

Summing up the difference between himself and his opponent, Sir Alec Douglas-Home, in the 1964 General Election:
'You might say that Alex is an amateur who can't control his professionals. Wilson is a professional who can't control his amateurs.'

At a meeting in Glasgow, a young man persistently interrupted his speech with shouts of 'Groundnuts'.
'There's an ageing Young Conservative ... His only contribution to the Blue Streak argument is to shout "Groundnuts" ... Where have you been, Rip van Winkle?'

Talk about splits in the Labour Party! Every time Mr Macmillan comes back from abroad, Mr Butler goes to the airport and grips him warmly by the throat.

In the middle of a discussion about religion, one of the group, which included Wilson, remarked, 'I do not believe in God.' Snapped back Wilson:
'I wonder if God believes in you?'

At the Labour Party Conference in 1975:
'I do not want to lead a party of zombies.'

Replying to Opposition demands for legislation on resale price maintenance the then Leader of the house, Mr Selwyn Lloyd, said: 'I have nothing to add. The Hon. Gentleman must draw his own con-clusions.'

Harold Wilson replied: 'If the Leader of the House has nothing to add, has he anything to subtract?'

On devaluation: 'From now on, the pound abroad is worth 14 per cent or so less in terms of other currencies. That doesn't mean, of course, that the pound here in Britain, in your pocket or purse or bank, has been devalued.'

HRH THE DUKE OF WINDSOR (1894-1972)

The thing that impresses me most about America is the way that parents obey their children.

Princely gifts don't come from princes any more. They come from tycoons.

BARONESS WOOTTON (1897-1988)

The rule used to be that men must work and women must weep. Women must now do both.

INDEX

89

90